The Bu

Once upon a time,
an old woman said,
"I am hungry.
I will make a bun."

So she got some flour.
She mixed it with milk.
She baked it in butter.

Then she put the bun
on the window sill to cool.

3

But then the bun jumped up.

It rolled off the window sill,
across the floor,
and out the door.

5

The old woman chased the bun,
but she could not catch it.

It rolled across the yard,
down the path,
under the gate,
and along the road.

It rolled along the road
until it met a rabbit.

"Little bun, little bun,
I will eat you up!"
said the rabbit.

9

"Please don't eat me," said the bun.
"I will sing you a song."

So the bun sang:
"I'm a bun, I'm a bun.
I was made from flour.
I was mixed with milk.
I was baked in butter.
I ran away from an old woman,
and I will run away from you, too."

The bun rolled along the road
until it met a bear.

"Little bun, little bun,
I will eat you up!"
said the bear.

"Please don't eat me," said the bun.
"I will sing you a song."

So the bun sang:
  "I'm a bun, I'm a bun.
  I was made from flour.
  I was mixed with milk.
  I was baked in butter.
  I ran away from an old woman.
  I ran away from a rabbit,
  and I will run away from you, too."

15

The bun rolled along the road until it met a fox.

"Little bun, little bun,
I will eat you up!"
said the fox.

16

"Please don't eat me," said the bun.
"I will sing you a song."

So the bun sang:
   "I'm a bun, I'm a bun.
   I was made from flour.
   I was mixed with milk.
   I was baked in butter.
   I ran away from an old woman.
   I ran away from a rabbit.
   I ran away from a bear,
   and I will run away from you, too."

"I can't hear you," said the fox.
"Come sit by my ear
and sing to me again."

21

So the bun jumped on the fox's head
and sang:
"I'm a bun, I'm a bun.
I was made from flour.
I was mixed with milk.
I was baked in butter.
I ran away from an old woman.
I ran away from a rabbit.
I ran away from a bear,
and I will run away from you, too."

Then the fox shook her head
and she ate the little bun in one SNAP!